7 Needs of
High Performing
Employees

*What Exceptional Workers
are Reluctant to Tell Management*

C.L. Holley

V1
12/28/2019

Cover photo by Andreas Klassen on Unsplash

ISBN: 9781652298151

Imprint: Independently published

Dedications

To my past and present outstanding leaders who have listened to my high performer concerns and responded positively to my needs. May you all continue to be excellent examples of visionary leaders.

John Hall – My former Manager
Rick Corn – My former VP/CIO
Wesley Cheplen – My current Director and Lead

Acknowledgments

To my awesome book editor, Angee Costa — author, speaker, and editor. Thanks for improving my writing and helping me clearly express my thoughts to readers.

Contents

Introduction

*E*ntrepreneur John Hall wrote a February 2019 article for Forbes entitled, *How You Can Keep High Performers Loyal to Your Company.* He states:

"Your star employees are arguably your company's biggest assets. These team members play a key role in the long-term health and success of your company. They're efficient, productive, and good for your bottom line, thanks to referrals and reduced turnover. But how can you keep high performers loyal?"

Keeping high performers loyal and happy is the premise of this book. One of the ways of doing so is to unearth and address issues they may be hesitant to share with leadership.

If you, as a business owner, executive, or manager, could get totally honest answers to the following question from your high performing employees, would you really want to hear their responses?

"What do you need to reach the next performance level?"

Your first impulse might be to listen with wide open ears. But then, would reservations surface? You may ponder:

What if the need is something I can't provide?

What if the need is something beyond my control?

What if the need is something about me that needs to change?

After thirty years of professional workplace experience as a high performer and leader, I've discovered there is an unwritten code of silence in which most employees, especially high performers, operate. The rule guarding this code is simple:

"If it can be held against me, I won't say it."

And for high performers, this can be multiplied by the fact that most of them have more to lose than underperformers.

What's the implication? There may be critical needs lurking in the far corners of the minds of your high performers that are pertinent to their continued growth and therefore, to the level of your company's success. As a visionary leader, you not only make strategic decisions from concrete data analysis, you also need to address issues that some employees may be reluctant to disclose. This book contains data from various studies and researches in conjunction with my thirty-year personal experience as a business professional.

To lead off, I want to share an experience I had years ago. I worked for a company that suffered from a high rate of employee turnover. Supervisors conducted employee meetings and tried to fish for answers but came up empty. Management held leadership think-tanks but found no solutions.

Finally, executives hired an external survey firm to produce online questionnaires with the promise that each employee's responses would be totally anonymous. It bombed out and was a huge failure. Why? The employees were fearful that their answers would somehow be linked back to their identity despite the promise of ambiguity. Those employees were very reluctant to share pertinent information for variety of reasons. It was the fear of reprisal, co-worker pressure, and not wanting to fall out of favor with leaders. Just the same, unshared critical information that hinders employee and company performance can be detrimental.

Through research and data analysis, many needs of high performers have been identified. This book focuses on seven of those needs. These needs were chosen for this book because, from my experience with hundreds of high performers over the past thirty years, these needs were the ones employees found most difficult to discuss with management.

In this book the following needs will be examined:

Need 1 Permission to Respectfully Disagree with Leadership

Need 2 Implementation of My Innovative Ideas

Need 3 Managerial Trust to do My Job.

Need 4 Other High Performers Around Me.

Need 5 Challenges that Drive Organizational Change

Need 6 Understanding of My Unique Challenges

Need 7 Understanding of My Unique Personality

As you read, each chapter will contain a section for self-reflection. Although you may provide some or all these needs, the important question to ask is:

Is the need fully provided? Does it flow from the top all the way down the leadership and management chain, directly to the high performer?

If there is doubt, perhaps it's time for a meeting of the minds of your leadership to ensure all needs are fully provided and available – without hindrance — by all your managers.

1

Permission to Respectfully Disagree with Leadership

*T*hink back a few days, weeks, or even months. Can you remember a time when an employee, including a leader reporting to you, suggested something different than your idea or instruction and communicated it directly to you? It would be very concerning if you went back six months or more and still came up empty. That could indicate your high performers may be operating in Yes, Sir or Yes,

Ma'am mode. They do what they're told, when they're told to do it, and how they're told to do it. No questions asked, no concerns raised, and no improvements suggested.

Perhaps they are afraid to respectfully speak up or push back with other ideas or suggestions because of the power of your position.

Position-related fear, where employees have a certain level of reservation about saying certain things to people in higher levels of authority, is a real workplace phenomena verified by case studies and surveys. In an online article of Harvard Business Review dated May 2007 entitled *Why Employees Are Afraid to Speak*, the authors share findings after interviewing 200 employees about the fear to speak up. Below was part of their conclusion:

"...yet half the employee respondents in a recent culture survey had revealed that they felt it was not "safe to speak up" or challenge traditional ways of doing things. What they were most reticent to talk about were not problems but rather creative ideas for improving products, processes, or performance. Why? In a phrase, self-preservation...Their frequent conclusion seemed to be,

"When in doubt, keep your mouth shut."

Could the self-preservation fear be an issue among your high performers? Is that the reason you're not getting respectful push back or alternative ideas?

That same article also revealed possible root causes for self-preservation including hostility from managers about past suggestions and broad vague perceptions about the work environment. While those findings aren't particularly surprising, it was their third finding that should cause leaders to really contemplate. It was unfounded speculation.

"Implicit, seemingly untested assumptions also led to silence. Many people reported withholding input from a person higher up in the corporate hierarchy because they believed (without any evidence) that the superior felt ownership of the project, process, or issue in question and would resent suggestions that implied a need for change. Employees also believed (again without direct experience) that their bosses would feel betrayed if constructive ideas for change were offered when more-senior leaders were present or that their bosses would feel embarrassed to be shown up by a subordinate in front of other subordinates."

The world of implication is filled with ghosts, goblins, and creeping things that tend to fuel workplace speculation. What is explicitly said can be very powerful, but what is implied can be even more powerful because it leaves room for the employee's imagination to run wild. Would your high performers have reservations about sharing constructive ideas with you that went against company norms or challenged traditional boundaries?

Years ago, I worked for an executive who was known for strictness and blunt methods of leading. There were times when I could see a better way of doing something and areas of possible improvements and savings. But because of this executive's stiff leadership style, I was very hesitant to suggest anything that contradicted the establishment. After several years, the executive and I were having a one-on-one conversation about communication with management. The executive said, "If you disagree with something I say, feel free to respectfully push back. I don't mind."

I was shocked and thought, I would have never guessed that in a million years if you hadn't told me.

Unfounded speculation about the executive's

reaction held me back from sharing several ideas for process improvement that could have saved the company thousands.

What about you? Do your high performers know they can respectfully disagree or offer alternative solutions without the fear of negative repercussions? If you have not explicitly communicated this to them, do you think they would be comfortable to suggest something different to you? If you're not sure of your answer, it may be time to have a conversation with them.

Solutions for Self-Preservation Fear

The article *Why Employees Are Afraid to Speak* offered several possible solutions that were all linked to explicitly inviting employees to share their ideas in an effort to challenge the myths and assumptions that fuel silence. The article stated:

"Our findings suggest that encouraging speech, therefore, isn't simply a matter of removing obvious barriers, such as a volatile leader or the threat of a summary dismissal (though that would help). Nor is it a matter of putting

formal systems in place, like hotlines and suggestion boxes. Making employees feel safe enough to contribute fully requires deep cultural change that alters how they understand the likely costs (personal and immediate) versus benefits (organizational and future) of speaking up."

That "deep cultural change" begins with:

- *Explicitly giving your high performers permission to respectfully disagree.*

Reassure them it's okay to share a different idea or method of doing something. Whatever they don't explicitly hear from you they will infer from a variety of sources including your leadership style and treatment of fellow employees. Here is an example of what can be communicated:

"It's okay to respectfully disagree with me or any other leader. We want to hear your opinions even if they contradict something leadership has suggested. The company needs everyone's innovative ideas—and that includes yours. We don't punish diversity of thought—we

welcome it."

The article contained the following that demonstrates the power of an employee's imagination:

"A culture of collective myths proved chilling—for example, stories of individuals who had said something in a public venue and then, as one R&D director put it, were "suddenly gone from the company."

The power of the rumor mill should not be underestimated. Steps should be taken to chase away the ghost whispers of why people disappear and the like. Leaders should share, both verbally and possibly in some written form, that employees will not disappear because they respectfully present an alternative idea or solution to management. By effectively communicating such facts, the power of the rumor mill will be diminished.

- Give them examples of what to say.

Assumptions should not be made that all high performers know what the word *respectfully* means when it comes to communication with upper management—especially when it comes to millennials and younger age groups. It would be wise to give them some examples of what to say and how to say it—teaching them to avoid comparative terms such as *better than* or *more than* when sharing ideas. For example:

Wrong way:

"I have a better idea than Fred's that will save the company much more money."

Right way:

"Sir or Ma'am. I would like to share an alternative idea if I may."

Just using the word *alternative* instead of *better* could prevent defensive behavior from management or co-workers. Words matter. And despite what many leaders say, wrong or insensitive words do hurt and tend to create a *defend myself and my ideas* mindset.

- *As a Leader, Beware of Negative Subliminal Statements (NSS)*

Subliminal messaging is a popular topic in the world of leadership. Simply put, it refers to statements or messages that carry a deeper meaning which will be received and understood by the hearer's subconscious. These hidden meanings can be good or bad based on the purpose of the speaker.

As an example, I once worked for a small business whose manager was very relaxed in her leadership approach. As a result, employees soon figured out they could goof off and half-perform with no consequences. When word of our team's poor performance reached upper management, she was replaced with a stern, hard-nosed manager. I'll never forget his words during our first team meeting.

"This is how things are going to work around here. It's my way or the highway!"

His tone and expressions were rough-and-tough, macho guy and his statements carried the subliminal messages of:

I alone determine what's done and how it's done. Just do what I say.

I don't want you to think about how to do something. Just do what I say.

Don't even think about sharing anything helpful with me. Just do what I say.

If you don't do what I say, I will fire you faster than you can blink.

I only stayed a couple more weeks after he took over, but I can still remember how eerily quiet and fearful my co-workers and I were as we followed his instructions to the letter. No one asked questions if they weren't sure about a task or process. They just guessed and hoped he wouldn't become angry and fire someone.

Subliminal statements don't have to be harsh like the one in my example. Sometimes they can be unintentional and occur as a result of familiar sayings such as:

I know this company like the back of my hand. This statement suggests the person knows the company so well that very few people can provide anything new or unknown.

I started with nothing and built this company from scratch. This statement may indicate the person sees himself or herself as the sole owner in all aspects, including ideas and innovations.

Both statements may be true, but what employees tend to glean from them may not be helpful in encouraging them to speak up. Also, those statements do not inspire inclusion that fosters a sense of invitation to the company. Rather, they are statements of exclusivity which suggest the company belongs — in all senses of the word — to the speaker and no one else can share in that ownership in any way. Therefore, wisdom instructs careful usage of words because words have power.

- Allow the Employees to Choose a Topic of Discussion

In most companies, agendas and topics for meetings are largely created by management with little or no input from employees. To improve more frequent, ongoing conversations, management could solicit team meeting topics from employees that are important to them. In doing so, they may bring issues to the discussion table that leaders may not be aware of or may not have addressed in a satisfactory manner. It would also help them to feel included in the development of workplace conversations which should improve their sense of inclusiveness.

The goal of this chapter is to unclog communication channels among your high performers. By addressing and removing obstacles to free speech, information will flow from employee to leader in a constructive manner that can improve relationships, trust, and hopefully, the company's bottom line.

Self-Reflection

Permission to Respectfully Disagree with Leadership

My leaders and employees know they can respectfully disagree with upper-level leaders.

[ ] Yes   [ ] No   [ ] Maybe

I am confident that all levels of management below me have communicated this message to their employees.

[ ] Yes   [ ] No   [ ] Maybe

My leaders and employees know how to respectfully disagree in ways that are sensitive and affirming.

[ ] Yes   [ ] No   [ ] Maybe

Notes/Thoughts:

To-Dos:

2

Implementation of My Innovative Ideas

Congratulations! Chapter one topics have been mastered in your organization. The communication faucet is fully opened, and conversation is uninhibited and freely flowing from your high performers to your leaders. By explicitly welcoming diversity of thoughts and opinion, a safe and respectful environment has been created that allows employees to share non-traditional, innovative ideas as well as untested theories on improving company performance.

Negative Subliminal Statements (NSS) have been

avoided along with using self-promoting words and phrases. Employees have been given freedom to contribute to meeting discussions by allowing them to add a topic of their choice to the meeting agenda.

The fear of self-preservation appears to be conquered and there is an increase in discussions both in team meetings and between co-workers in the workplace. Unfounded speculations are no longer an issue. Your high performers are sharing their thoughts and even their fears with leadership. That's great! But what now?

There is a saying in the plumbing profession that goes something like this:

If you turn on the faucet, be prepared to deal with all the water!

Are you ready to address and possibly implement the ideas, concerns, and suggestions of your high performers? The remainder of this chapter will be dedicated to sharing constructive ways to keep the flow of communication open by eventually implementing some of the good innovative ideas of your high performers.

There are situations and circumstances that may cause employees to stop talking—including failure of management to implement any good ideas high performers bring forward. Certainly, not all ideas will be implemented. But at some point, management should implement some of their innovative brainstorms. After all, that is why your employees poured out their thoughts to management—to experience the result of seeing their ideas not only recognized but assimilated into organizational practice and company policy.

Avoid Pseudo Voice

When leaders ask employees for their input but never intend to act on it, a condition is developed in the workplace called *Pseudo Voice*. In the Leadership section of *Strategy+Business*, an article entitled *When Employees Talk and Managers Don't Listen*, dated September 2011, describes it.

"The researchers refer to the illusion of having

participative influence as "pseudo voice." It comes into play whenever a manager ignores ideas slipped into suggestion boxes, concerns voiced in meetings, and complaints registered in employee surveys. And it is common even at companies that say they are committed to giving employees a chance to contribute their ideas."

In some companies, management may solicit employee feedback and contributions but have no intentions of taking their input seriously enough to consider implementation. Leaders may take notations in their agenda books, listen as employees communicate their innovative ideas, but at the end of the day, fail to follow up on any promises of examining their information.

Pseudo Voice is given by some leaders to give employees the belief that their voices are being heard and their ideas and opinions matter. But the problem with this approach is sooner or later, the employees figure it out. In the same article, the author writes:

"Dangers lurk if suggestions are sought but are not considered... If employees conclude that a manager is just trying to win points by paying lip service to consulting

them — and has no intention of acting on their advice —
they are likely to stop offering input and, worse, act out
their frustration by clashing with their colleagues."

As an example, from personal experience, some years ago an upper level manager in my department put out a request for the development of a tracking mechanism for technical projects. I accepted the challenge and proceeded, with the manager's input and feedback, to create the mechanism. I was proud of the hard work and creativity that went into its formulation.

After releasing it and making it available to other co-workers, it was never utilized by anyone else other than myself. In fact, the manager who requested it never referenced it and never suggested its usage to other teams. I was very disappointed that the manager really had no intention of using it. It was a clear case of pseudo voice.

As mentioned earlier in this chapter, not all ideas and suggestions from high performers should be implemented. Some may not be conducive to the company. Others may be untested and present an unreasonable level of organizational risk. Other suggestions may have been attempted in the past with disastrous results.

In these situations, leaders should carefully explain the pros and cons of the ideas, pointing out the rewards verses the risks, and always end the discussion by encouraging the employee to continue bringing ideas. In the arena of public speaking, this type of feedback is known as the *sandwich approach* — start with encouragement, share the cons of the idea and why it might not work, and end with more encouragement for continued communication.

But in all cases, management should have the sincere intention of examining and addressing every innovative idea or concern voiced by high performers. That means, at some point, implementing a good idea to prove to employees that their input is taken seriously.

Here is another finding in that same article:

"...employees who thought their manager was indeed paying attention spoke up more often and got along better with one another, improving the organization's functioning as a whole."

Avoiding the pseudo voice effect by explaining details about problem solutions and implementing some good suggestions can lead to improved organizational functioning. It can build trust between high performers and leadership. It can even improve relationships between co-workers by promoting a healthy competitive environment where employees are actively searching for improvements in company operations. And it all begins with the intentions of management—to sincerely evaluate and act on good innovative ideas and suggestions from high performers.

But you are not a pseudo-leader. You are a visionary next level leader searching for methods to improve employee and company performance. In fact, you probably are reading this book because the subtitle, *What Exceptional Workers are Reluctant to Tell Management*, attracted your attention. You wanted to know the hidden thoughts and opinions on the minds of your high performers. And because you wanted to know, I'm confident you are also willing to address them—the bad and the good.

It also may be a good idea to make sure pseudo voice is not occurring on any managerial or leadership level downstream in your organization.

- If Needed, Establish an Idea Evaluation Infrastructure (IEI)

Your high performers are sharing ideas and management is committed to evaluating all and acting on some of those suggestions. But is there an infrastructure in place to carry out the process of evaluating, testing, and determining of viability?

Odds are your organization already has a formal process, procedure, or system in place to determine if or when new solutions are integrated into current operations. If that is the case, is it flexible enough to allow for non-standard, non-company-traditional innovative ideas and suggestions your high performers may introduce?

All evaluation processes should include answers for the following questions or situations:

- What is the process for introducing a new innovative idea or suggestion?
  Online form? Verbal communication with manager? Etc.

- Who will be involved in evaluating and testing (if needed) the new idea?
  Manager and submitter? Evaluation team? Etc.

- What are the guidelines to determine viability of the new idea?
  Cost? Revenue? Risk? Process, Product, or Production Improvement?

- When and how will upper management be notified and/or included in evaluation of new idea? Before testing? After conclusion of Successful tests? Etc.

An Idea Evaluation Infrastructure (IEI) should not be complicated, rigid, or burdensome and overloaded with paperwork. But it does need the ability to capture and store the basic information about what the idea is, who presented it, any testing details including the results of those tests, and whether it was implemented. A good IEI has the potential to do two things:

(1) *Provide guidelines for high performers to formulate and introduce innovative ideas to management.*

(2) *Serve as documentation and database of all*

evaluated suggestions to prevent repeating ideas that didn't work.

If your high performers know there is a formal system or process in place, its existence can increase their confidence and trust that management will take their ideas seriously.

- Empower Lower Level Managers to Act on Input

Your high performers are talking and there is a formal or informal IEI in place. But for some reason, implementation actions on several great suggestions are not being pursued. What could be the problem? Perhaps the problem exists with lower level managers and leaders.

In some organizations, there are lower level leaders who are stuck in their own ways of doing things and are married to the current organizational structure, no matter how rigid and dysfunctional. But this isn't the case with your organization. Your lower level managers and leaders have bought into the importance of high performer input and are excited about its potential. So why the failure to implement?

There is an interesting article in the Harvard Business Review entitled, *Research: Why Managers Ignore Employees' Ideas*, dated April 08, 2019, that contains the following:

"We found that managers face two distinct hurdles: They are not empowered to act on input from below, and they feel compelled to adopt a short-term outlook to work."

The article is based on a recent paper published at Organizational Science and drew some conclusions all leaders should examine closely. When it comes to your lower level managers and leaders, are they empowered to make needed changes without going through a tedious central approval process, and do they have a long-term orientation plan?

Here is a hypothetical example:

Sarah is a front-line manager overseeing product production and domestic shipments. She loves the organization and is committed to employee engagement and company performance. Over the past three years, a few high performers have suggested great ideas in the production and shipment process that she's convinced could improve long-term company performance. But because she's constantly pushed to reach short-term goals and does not have autonomy to make changes without going through a rigorous and time-consuming process at HQ, her high performers' ideas are noted, but never pursued.

One can understand why Sarah would not be compelled to pursue implementation of her high performers' suggestions. She is in a very uncomfortable position. She values the employee's ideas and would love to put them into practice. However, the reality of her short-term responsibility and the lack of power to change things make it almost impossible to pursue implementation. This is reflected in the article:

"They experience centralized decision structures, in which authority lies at the top of the hierarchy, and they are merely "go-betweens." And even when they are empowered to act, they still confront demands to show success in the short-term rather than look out for longer-term sustainability."

According to the article, a study was done with 160 students acting as managers, where some were given autonomy and others very rigid task instructions. Student-managers with low autonomy indicated they would allocate 25% less time discussing work issues with their employees compared to high autonomy student-managers.

In another study with 424 working adults who were given similar situations with high and low autonomy, managers in low empowerment conditions were 30% less likely to seek feedback from their employees as compared to high autonomy managers.

Perhaps the most significant study was done concerning the combination of high autonomy and long-term orientation (tendency to give greater weight to long-term outcomes). Using the same 424 managers, the study found the managers sought input from below only when they were *both* empowered and favored long-term success of their team.

The article concluded with this:

"We tend to blame managers when they fail to create

speak-up cultures. We say that their ego or fear of change prevents them from encouraging voice from employees. But our findings indicate that it is unreasonable to ask managers to solicit and encourage ideas and input from employees when they are not empowered themselves and are asked to focus on short-term outcomes."

Could your lower level managers and leaders be in the same or similar position as Sarah? If so, how can you as a leader, help your lower level managers and leaders have more autonomy and adopt a long-term company success orientation in addition to a short-term view?

Organizations should examine their practices regarding management and leadership. Is there too much micromanagement that may impede lower level managers' and leaders' sense of autonomy? Are long-term views being emphasized and discussed along with short-term responsibilities? Improving both could significantly increase the effectiveness of lower level leaders and high performers and the bottom-line company performance.

Self-Reflection

Implementation of My Innovative Ideas

My lower level managers and leaders have a certain level of autonomy to make needed and proven changes without going through a rigorous centralized process with upper management.

[ ] Yes   [ ] No   [ ] Maybe

My lower level managers and leaders have short term responsibilities, but also have a long-term view of company sustainability.

[ ] Yes   [ ] No   [ ] Maybe

I and my lower level leaders are aware of the dangers of pseudo voice and make efforts to avoid committing it.

[ ] Yes   [ ] No   [ ] Maybe

Notes/Thoughts:

To-Dos:

3

Managerial Trust to do My Job

*I*n a report on Employee Job Satisfaction and Engagement by the Society for Human Resource Management (p. 27), a survey was conducted in November-December 2015 of 600 U.S. employees, and found 55% rated Trust between employee and senior management as very important. Similarly, in the Harvard Business Review for July 2017, an article entitled *Want Your Employees to Trust You? Show You Trust Them*, made this point:

"Executives and managers invest a lot of effort and time building trust in their teams: both establishing trust in their employees and ensuring that their employees trust them in return. But many employees say they do not feel trusted by their managers. And when employees don't feel trusted, workplace productivity and engagement often suffer. It's up to managers to signal trust in their employees in consistent and thoughtful ways."

Several years ago, I had an exit interview for a company. I tried to convince myself it was no big deal, but when I sat in the office of the HR manager, my entire body tensed up—so much that my hands formed a death grip on the side of the chair.

"I know you might be hesitant to open up about your work experience." The HR manager said. "But I encourage you to be honest. I already know there are issues in your department. I just want to know the truth."

I took a deep breath and said, "Okay. I will be open and honest."

For the next forty-five minutes, I opened up about the severe distrust I felt coming from some in leadership—giving specific examples and sharing why those managerial acts made me feel extremely untrusted. I ended with a question,

"Why hire me and not trust me to do my job?"

The HR manager understood the importance of trust from upper level leaders and said, "I know how important trust is in my position. One of the reasons I am happy and fulfilled in this capacity is because I know my upper level leader trusts me to do my job. I'm sorry your past years of experience here have not been the same."

My leaders did not explicitly say they didn't trust me. It was several things they *did* that made me *feel* untrusted.

- It was the constant questioning and doubting of my evaluations and opinions — to the point of dismissing them or consistently seeking a second source for re-evaluations.

- It was the assigning of complex projects that I was hired to do over to outside expertise.

- It was having private discussions and making decisions about areas of my responsibilities without my knowledge or input.

- It was the false accusation from an upper level manager that I had done something wrong on a computer system that caused a one-day outage.

Can you understand why I felt that way? In the same article, in a section with the subtitle, *Does Your Team Feel Trusted? 7 Questions for Managers*, these questions are posed for leaders to ponder:

- Do I show my employees that I feel confident in Their skills?

- Do I show my employees that I care about their welfare?

- Do I show my employees that I think they are capable of performing their jobs?

- Do I give my employees influence over the things that affect them most in the workplace?

- Do I give my employees the opportunity to take part in making job-related decisions that affect them?

- Do I encourage my employees to take risks?

- Do my words and deeds convey how much I trust my employees?

These questions are deep soul searchers for leaders. The remainder of this chapter will focus on identifying signs of managerial distrust and ways leaders can foster trust in their employees.

Signs of Managerial Distrust

- Micromanaging Employees

Exercising excessive and unnecessary control over an employee's job functions, assignments, or work environment signals a lack of trust. It often leaves high performers feeling boxed in, stifled, or severely limited in what they can do and how they can do it. In these situations, there is little to no room for employees to use their creativity, innovation, or imagination in developing alternative solutions or methods.

At the heart of most micromanagement tendencies is the fear leaders experience that employees might make them look bad. That fear can be rooted in self-pride.

Some examples of micromanagement are:

- Unnecessary and unreasonable accounting of employee's time.

- Excessive and unwarranted updates and changes to employee's projects or reports under the guise of *correction.*

- Constant and unneeded tweaking of employee's work not according to company or industry standards, but according to manager's standards or preferences.

When micromanaging occurs, high performers often feel untrusted and fail to reach the level of responsibility and independence needed to become critical decision makers. Instead, the tendency is to only do what the manager or leaders says — exactly the way he or she says it. It tends to create a work force that are *doers only*, not thinkers.

- Unreasonable Refusal to Give Employees Higher Responsibilities

Very few things signal trust as well as responsibility with things of high importance. This holds true not only for things of the company, but also things related to the reputation of the leader.

Whenever managers fail to give high profile projects or assignments to certain employees, it's usually because he or she believes the employee is incapable of performing the duties to a high standard. This could be justified by management due to a lack of training or lack of personal character on the employee's part. But when the refusal is unreasonable such that an employee who does have necessary training and ability is being stonewalled, it can suggest a lack of trust by leaders.

- Unnecessarily Omitting Employees from Discussions, Decisions, and Input Related to Their Areas of Responsibility.

Collaboration can be a powerful promoter of trust. When high performers are invited to contribute in the discussions and decisions concerning their areas of responsibilities, it tends to strengthen their trust in management and increase their level of confidence. However, to be purposefully overlooked or ignored by leadership when one should be included can send a strong suggestion that management may not be interested in or confident in the high performer's thoughts, suggestions, or input.

An invitation to collaborate can also be viewed by employees as a sign of respect from management. As proof of this power of relationship aspect, the *Society for Human Resource management* has a 2016 survey and report entitled, *Employee Job Satisfaction and Engagement: Millennials: Misunderstood in the Workplace?*

The research report concluded the top four job satisfaction contributors for millennials and, surprisingly, the top contributor wasn't compensation. The top four were:

(66%) Respectful Treatment of all Employees at all
     Levels
(65%) Compensation
(61%) Benefits
(58%) Job Security

This research report suggests leaders and management should give more credence and importance to relationship-oriented aspects such as building and enhancing trust—not just for millennials, but for all employees.

* * *

Solutions to Foster Trust in Employees

Although trust cannot be quantified, intentionally fostering it can have a huge impact on high performers. Because it is necessary for employees to *feel* trusted, there is a certain amount of human perspective involved. Some employees may perceive certain managerial acts as indications of distrust while other employees may overlook them for various reasons.

Setting aside such situations, here is what Welltower human capital specialist Michael Schneider wrote in a July 2018 article for Inc. com, entitled, *An 8-Year Study Reveals the Key to a High-Performing Culture – and 8 Ways to Build It.*

"You can invest in the latest technology, lean out processes, and add as many extra employee incentives as you want. However, if you're going to motivate your workforce and create a high-performing organization, then you'll need a component that can't be bought--trust."

In the article, he references a fascinating brain-activity study conducted to measure trust by Paul J. Zak, author and professor of economic sciences, psychology, and management at Claremont Graduate University. Here is summary of Zak's findings:

"Zak found that when compared to those in the lowest quartile, people working in high-trust organizations are 76 percent more engaged, 50 percent more productive, and 50 percent more likely to stay."

Knowing the high importance of trust, specifically the trust a manager has toward an employee, and the company benefits that a healthy level of trust can provide, here are a few things leaders can do to foster trust in their employees.

- Utilize Clear Directions and Guidance

Leaders and managers should utilize clear directions and guidance coupled with an open-door policy for employees to ask questions and receive clarification. When employees have a clear set of instructions and expectations, it tends to reduce misunderstandings — which can also be a source of distrust.

But these directions and guidance should not be unnecessarily strict and rigid as to kill high performers' innovative creativity. If there is a more productive method or cost saving way of performing a task, leaders should leave room for employees to discover it.

- Engage in Open and Honest Conversation

By using open, honest, and prompt communication,

leaders have the power to reduce anxiety among employees and build trust. However, studies show general communication with employees is something many leaders struggle with.

In a January 2018 article of Government Executive entitled, *Almost 70% of U.S. Managers Are Scared to Talk to Their Employees*, author Corrinne Purtill writes:

"In 2016, a survey of more than 2,000 U.S. adults (paywall) asked managers what they found most difficult about communicating with employees. Some 37% of managers said they found it hard to give negative feedback to workers about their performance, 20% said they struggled to share their own vulnerability, and another 20% disliked being the messenger for company policies. But a full 69% of respondents said that they found "communicating in general" to be the hardest part about communicating with employees."

Managers' problems with communication can lead to high performers feeling less engaged. Regular and meaningful communication is one of the primary things employees say they need to feel engaged and productive at work. According to the same article, in the most recent Gallup survey of the U.S. workplace, the company's annual in-depth report on more than 31 million workers across US industries, 67% of workers say they're not engaged at work. Could the 69% of managers who have problems communicating have any connection with the 67% of employees who don't feel engaged?

To demonstrate, years ago, I was working for a company and sitting in my manager's office talking about a system situation. I asked about third party access to our systems and shared some concerns I had with giving them such high level accounts. Before I asked, I knew by word of mouth and by my own investigation why they were given such access, but I wanted to hear it from my manager. I was very disappointed to hear the response given because it wasn't truthful. As a result, I lost respect and trust for the manager.

Openness and honesty are more important than the news being shared. Even if it's bad news, employees will appreciate it more if their leaders and managers are straightforward — especially with negative information that could have an impact on their employment situation.

- When Applicable, Give Employees More Responsibility with Important Tasks

At a company I previously worked for, management was accustomed to bringing in third party vendors and consultants to perform high profile projects. One project was done every three years with the same outside consultants despite having company employees with technical expertise. Word of mouth spread, and rumors circulated that management wanted someone to blame in case something went wrong.

That may not have been true, but the lack of confidence shown by management was certainly felt by those employees who wanted the challenge and the responsibility of doing high profile projects.

Refusing to allow employees to carry out certain aspects of their jobs that management may deem too risky is a sign of distrust. Leaders may have distrust in the employee's knowledge, experience, or competence. And yes, there are some employees who may not be ready for more responsibility. But for those who are, especially high performers, it's critical to build their trust by assigning them high impact tasks for which they are trained to perform.

Leaders would do well if they offered authority and ownership to employees by handing out tasks and assignments with high level impact. Obviously, this should be undergirded with clear instructions and avenues for employees to get clarification on questionable tasks. By delegating important tasks to high performers, leaders are empowering them to take more responsibility and pride in their work.

Chapter Conclusion

Years ago, I worked for a company but had never led a project of importance. I had a conversation with my executive leader expressing the desire for more responsibility. On the next project, I was given the lead and after working very hard, was instrumental in leading the team to complete the high-profile task without incident.

Afterwards, one of the leaders shared a comment from a manager during a meeting:

"What did you do to Charlie?" the manager asked the executive. "Seems like someone lit a fire under him?"

The manager didn't know I asked the executive for a chance to do bigger things and for more responsibility. Because I was a high performer, I was uncomfortable seeing others do work I was hired to do. Till that point, management had never asked if I could do the task. Could that be the case with some of your high performers?

Self-Reflection
Managerial Trust to do My Job

My employees, especially my high performers, know they have my managerial trust.

[ ] Yes   [ ] No   [ ] Maybe

Employees of my leaders also know their managers trust them to do their jobs.

[ ] Yes   [ ] No   [ ] Maybe

I communicate the trust I have in my leaders and employees in different ways.

[ ] Yes   [ ] No   [ ] Maybe

Notes/Thoughts:

To-Dos:

4

Other High Performers Around Me

*I*n a piece for Forbes magazine dated February 2019, entrepreneur and author John Hall wrote an article entitled, *How You Can Keep High Performers Loyal To Your Company.* He contended:

"Don't allow your top performers to be surrounded by low performers or people with bad attitudes. This can drain their morale, energy, and productivity and make them feel they're carrying others' burdens on top of their own."

I can attest. Early in my career, I worked for an

emerging manufacturing company. I was focused and dedicated to top level job performance, and it was reflected in my actions in the workplace. One day, the manager called an emergency team meeting with our group that numbered around twenty or so employees.

As I walked toward the meeting room, the manager gently nudged me on the shoulder and said, "Not you, Charlie. No need for you to hear this. You can continue your work."

I didn't know whether to be encouraged or worried. After the meeting, a co-worker told me what it was all about. "He cut into us about slacking off in general and about taking too much time in the break room." He said. "Looks like you were the only one he spared."

I was partly happy and relieved, but I was also worried about co-worker resentment. What would the others think of me? Would they think I was trying to show them up? Would they view me as a bosses' boy or kiss-up? In the following weeks of that episode, several co-workers' attitude toward me changed from friendly to cracking off-hand jokes and purposely avoiding me.

I remember the awful way I felt—lonely and like a fish out of water. I wondered why I was the only person out of a group of twenty-something people who wanted to excel in performance. I longed for someone else, another high performer I could connect with, to join the team. But it didn't happen and eventually I left the company.

Author Alex Palmer wrote a research article in January 2014 for Incentive Magazine entitled, Co-Workers Are Most Important Factor for Workplace Happiness. The article states:

"While managers are vital for an employee's success and sense of place in an organization, a new study finds that co-workers play a more important role in ensuring a worker's happiness at her job....Prominent among their findings is that employee happiness is 23.3 percent more correlated to connections with co-workers than with direct supervisors."

I can certainly identify with the research findings. Now, in hindsight, I believe being the only high performer in my group hurt my morale and my performance. There were times when I hated to come to work and days when the loneliness seemed to take its toll. I left the company within a year of that incident and don't know how the continued isolation would have affected me in the long run—both personally and professionally.

In the same article, Palmer references a study by *TINYPulse Engagement Survey* of over 40,000 responses from more than 300 worldwide companies, where the correlation coefficient between employees' happiness and their relationships with co-workers was 0.92 compared to only 0.74 for employees with their managers.

This finding suggests who employees work with carries more weight than who they answer to. The article shares the top five things respondents loved about their jobs:

- *Immediate Team and Colleagues*
- *Freedom/Responsibility*
- *Culture/Atmosphere*
- *Variety/Learning*
- *Challenges*

Relationships with co-workers carry more weight

because more time is spent with co-workers than with managers, supervisors, or executives. Co-workers sit together, eat together, and troubleshoot together as well as carry out assignments together. In light of this, it is important to have co-workers who can collaborate and communicate.

This is reflected in the same article with the following responses to this question: *What are workers looking for in their fellow team members:*

Collaboration/Communication: 44.3 %

Knowledge Skills and Talents: 26.4 %

Positive Attitude: 24.5 %

Fun: 4.8 %

The article summarizes with this statement:

"This provides a blueprint for smart human resources and executive teams to screen and hire for these traits to create a group of high performers that attract and retain other high performers," writes the report's authors.

As a leader, you may be familiar with the concept of like-attracts-like when it comes to professional relationships. High performers tend to collaborate and communicate best with other high performers. High achievers prefer to team up with other high achievers because they often share similar work ethics, passion to excel, and goal-oriented workplace performance. Therefore, it is important for employees to have at least one co-worker with whom they feel professional kindred — someone with similar drive to excel.

In the opening example of my experience, this friendly comradery was what I lacked. The remainder of this chapter will focus on possible ways leaders can establish or expand an environment with multiple high performers — a place where high achievers can thrive and grow together.

Ways to Build/Enhance High Performer Teams

- Hire Other High Performers

The most obvious way to establish or expand a high

performer team environment is by hiring other high performers. Research offers several definitions of who is considered a high performer. For this book's sake, the four characteristics found in John Hall's article (stated at the beginning of this chapter) will be used: *How can you spot high performers?* Here are a few giveaways:

They do more than just accomplish goals. They request additional assignments and look for new opportunities to push their limits and develop new skills.

They're proactive. They don't wait for you to sign them up for an online course, conference, or training session. They'll often do this on their own — even if they must pay for it out of pocket.

They seek feedback. They ask you for performance reviews and want to know how they're doing so they can improve and become more self-aware.

They consistently deliver high-quality work. High performers aren't content with completing an assignment just to get it done. They make sure it meets their high standards before submitting it.

For managers and leaders to determine if potential candidates possess some or most of these qualities, questions beyond those found on typical job applications should be utilized. Most standard applications are designed to highlight a person's talent and potential—not their tendency to be high performers. In order to discover that, it will be necessary to delve deeper into a person's character and thought process. Here are some examples of probing questions that can uncover high performer potential:

Are you goal-oriented? If so, tell me about a recent goal you set and any challenges you may have encountered.

Do you like learning and growing? Tell me about something you recently learned and how you learned it.

What types of people do you prefer to work with?

Those who do the minimum to get by or those who are driven to perfection?

Give me a few words or phrases that describe your character. (Listen for words that describe high performer traits such as goal oriented, love for learning, etc.)

I once worked at a company that had a great team that consisted of several high performers. But after a new manager hired a new team member with very little experience or drive to excel, one of the high performers confided in me.

"I don't believe this!" he said in disgust. "I don't have time to baby-sit anyone! This new hire knows nothing and doesn't seem interested in learning!"

Situations like this — high performers feeling as if they must carry unnecessary loads of other employees — are what the article described. But they can be avoided by hiring other high performers to establish or enhance your team.

- Assign a High Performer to Mentor a Non-High Performer

This doesn't imply your team has only two types of groups—high performers and non-high performers. It is likely you have employees that don't fit neatly into either group. They may be somewhere in the middle and perform satisfactorily but aren't standouts in a specific skill. But you have identified those with above average performance and by mentoring them with average or below average performers, there is the potential to bring underachievers up to the high performance level.

However, this takes a willing employee—one who wants to learn and grow and who will not be offended or intimidated by becoming a mentee to another coworker. There is a saying in the sports world that goes something like this:

"If you hang around winners, you will become a winner."

There is truth to this belief, and I have personally witnessed it happen in a few instances over my career. Although there is no guarantee that mentoring arrangements will succeed, the potential advantage of seeing an employee rise to the level of high performer should far outweigh the risks.

- Invest in a Potential High Performer

The word *investment* implies getting a greater return than what was spent. Some employees may have the drive and the desire to excel but not the skill set. He or she may need training, coaching, or even encouraging. Perhaps if you explicitly tell him or her, *I'm willing to invest in you if you are willing to learn and grow*, it may be just the thing that employee needs to jump-start a promising career as a high performer.

There is a real fear among managers that if they significantly invest in training and other tangibles for employees, there is a possibility they may leave for another company. That is certainly true. But it is also possible they will stay, become more productive, and be instrumental in increasing the bottom line of the company. As they say in the world of investments: If you can't afford to lose the money—don't invest.

But I have developed and live by a simple motto over my career—one that I've seen work often:

TRAIN Them and TRUST Them.

Self-Reflection

Other High Performers Around Me

My high performers have other high performers around them.

[ ] Yes   [ ] No   [ ] Maybe

I have at least one underperforming employee who may rise to high performer level if mentored or trained.

[ ] Yes   [ ] No   [ ] Maybe

I have at least one high performer who would be a good mentor for underperformers.

[ ] Yes   [ ] No   [ ] Maybe

Notes/Thoughts:

To-Dos:

5

Challenges That Drive Organizational Change

he Society for Human Resource Management has a research report based on 2016 information, entitled Employee Job Satisfaction and Engagement: Revitalizing a Changing Workforce. In the research report, 47% of employees rated meaningfulness of job as important and 42% rated their current job as somewhat satisfied. (p 31-32)

To further explain their definition of *meaningfulness of job*, the report contains this:

"The work itself (e.g., stimulating and challenging assignments) can enhance engagement as employees are more motivated to explore tasks that incite curiosity and inspiration... Rather than mundane, repetitive tasks, employees often prefer working on topics that inspire and energize them; even better, if employees are given the freedom to decide what projects are completed and how. "

Many leaders understand the importance of assigning stimulating and challenging work to high performers. The problem occurs when that task or project comes with high visibility and impact to the company and leadership. For example, if an IT project fails, the entire application user community will be down for an extended period and all upper management will blame the immediate manager for the outage.

With such pressure facing leaders, it is understandable why some supervisors might choose to forgo using their high performers and opt to bring in professional consultants. But what does that lack of faith do to employees? It sends a strong message that the supervisor does not trust them. And that can lead to lower morale and a lack of opportunity for professional growth and development. Moreover, a dependency is usually developed upon using outside assistance while employees fail to grow through learning and doing.

The short answer for this dilemma, as communicated in a previous chapter, is to train them and trust them —not only with less important tasks, but also with meaningful high profile and high-risk projects that drive change.

This is particularly true of high performers. Chaka Booker, Managing Director for The Broad Center, wrote an April 2019 article entitled What Makes High Performers Shine So Bright? You do. In the article he states:

"High performers are usually developed in these areas, so give them challenges that specifically require them to drive change. Implementing change is high risk, high return and incredibly complex — perfect for developing your high performers."

I mentioned in a previous chapter about my experience working for a company whose managers constantly brought in outside professional consultants to perform certain high profile and high-risk projects. While that may have been convenient for management, it was disheartening for employees—especially high performers such as myself. I craved the challenge and the opportunity to learn and grow. I wanted the greater level of responsibility and the satisfaction of accomplishing something big.

But leaders did not ask if employees were capable of doing the job. After several years of the same, workplace morale continued to slip until many employees, including myself, decided to seek growth opportunity elsewhere.

What may be more disheartening is it didn't appear leadership saw the signs of employee discontentment. Even after several good employees left, no major changes took place to address the issues that caused the low morale.

In a January 2019 article for HR Dive entitled *Why are your top performers leaving?* author Riia O'Donnell writes:

"Some signals may hint at a great employee getting ready to move on. "The most obvious is a lack of engagement," Moulton said. A manager may see performance dips, lack

of interest, or even complaints they are overwhelmed."

In my case, it was a fear of job loss. Months after my hire at a company, one leader said during a casual conversation, "This is a right to work state. I don't need a reason to fire anyone."

That statement led me to believe improving worker retention wasn't high on that leader's list of priorities. That may not have been the case, but those words did not improve employee confidence in management.

If you have high performers, are you seeing any of the warning signs of employee discontentment? The following sections will focus on possible solutions.

Solutions for High Performer Discontentment

- Consistent Communication

High performers are interested in what they need to do to accomplish goals and how they are doing between projects. That means leaders should constantly communicate tasks and project milestones, progress, and ways they can improve performance. It's critical for high performers to receive meaningful feedback from leadership and to have an open-door policy with management. Leaders should not wait for performance review time to chart goals and give high performers valuable information.

- SMART Business Goals

According to a blog article entitled High-performers in the workplace: How to Identify and Develop you're A-Team, written in July 2018 for Rallyware (News and thoughts on Workforce Engagement), the author says:

"While setting business goals for high-performers to achieve, make sure that these goals are SMART (specific, measurable, achievable, relevant, and time-bound)."

The point is made that goals too easy to achieve could lead high performers to boredom and goals too difficult to achieve could lead to employee burnout and frustration. Therefore, goals should be in-between—challenging enough to spark and retain high performer interest, yet attainable so employees can finish and celebrate.

- Opportunities to Drive Change

Leaders should offer high performers opportunities to work on high profile and high-risk projects and tasks. This should only be done when they have the proper training and experience or the proper support. Managers should also solicit their input whenever high impact situations arise. That would indicate trust from management.

- The Choice of Their Next Challenge

Allowing high performers to choose their next challenge takes the guess work out of finding tasks that will inspire them. Leaders can rest assured high performers will choose something interesting and challenging as well as ensure a sense of ownership for the project. Also, the freedom of choice can give the high performer increased trust in management.

Keeping high performers engaged, challenged, and

fulfilled can be very difficult. However, if leaders implement some or all these previous solutions, there is a greater chance that high achievers will remain and flourish.

Self-Reflection

Challenges That Drive Organizational Change

I allow my employees and leaders to take responsibility for and work on high impact projects that drive organizational change.

[ ] Yes   [ ] No   [ ] Maybe

I allow my leaders and employees to choose some of their workplace project challenges.

[ ] Yes   [ ] No   [ ] Maybe

I and my leaders set organizational goals that are SMART (specific, measurable, achievable, relevant, and time-bound).

[ ] Yes   [ ] No   [ ] Maybe

Notes/Thoughts:

To-Dos:

6

Understanding of My Unique Challenges

*L*et's assume you've mastered the previous chapters and have succeeded in building an outstanding team where no less than 35% are high performers. According to Personnel Psychology's February 2012 issue, an article entitled, *The Best and the Rest: Revisiting the Norm of Normality of Individual Performance* cites a study that indicates high performers, on average, achieve 400% more than average employees.

If this holds true with your company and teams, your group containing 35% high performers should demonstrate significantly higher output and performance. But in your case, only a modest increase in bottom line expansion is noticed – nowhere near the expected additional output. What could be the problem?

While having high performers on any team is great, various case studies have revealed unique issues related to this group of super achievers. These are problems that can severely hinder or reduce their productivity and thus, team and company productivity. All employees have problems in the workplace. However, the ones shared in the remainder of this chapter tend to happen with high performers at a greater rate.

Identifying and correcting these unique challenges that I refer to as high performance killers could enable leaders to enhance the company bottom line by a level proportional to the number of high performers on teams.

Unique High Performer Challenges

- High Performers May Face Coworker Resentment

Unfortunately, another one of the negatives that come with being a top performer is that everyone on the team may not see the high performer's outstanding achievements in a positive light. Peers may belittle, insult, or even damage the reputation of high performers because they resent their superstar status that often comes with rewards, recognition, and promotions.

In a July 2017 article for Scientific American entitled, The Problem with Being a Top Performer, author Francesca Gino wrote:

" ...new research demonstrates that performing at high levels can also come with some heavy costs: it can make our peers resent us and try to undermine our good work. And there's more: the "social penalty" that star performers suffer is actually higher in more collaborative workplaces."

It's not uncommon for high performers to become targets of co-workers' jealously and envy. Therefore, leaders should watch for signs of co-worker sabotage or even displeasure that can stem from resentment.

Some signs to watch for are:

Social Isolation: Refusing to socialize with and encouraging others to ignore the high performer.

Unnecessary Competition: Continuously comparing ones' work to that of a high performer often placing it in a more favorable light.

Character Assassination: Constantly saying and implying untrue things about a high performer to stain his or her reputation.

When a leader encounters these or other signs of co-worker resentment, it is best to speak to the heart of the offending employee to help him or her view the high performer as an asset that brings benefits to everyone.

- High Performers can Intimidate Other Employees

There is truth to the statement, *Talent can intimidate*. It's true in athletics, academics, and in business. The brightest and most talented employees tend to intimidate less talented employees who may have lower self-esteem and a less ambitious work ethic. Comparing oneself with others is a natural human inclination. Therefore, when a 50% performance employee compares himself or herself to a 400% high performer, it's only natural for him or her to feel less vital to the importance of the team. Lower level performers may even harbor a sense of inferiority in terms of talent and ability.

According to a November 2014 article in *the Harvard Business Review* entitled *What High Performers Want at Work*, author Karle Willyerd writes:

"A high performer can deliver 400% more productivity than the average performer. That means top talent produces 4X as much as the average employee, and companies like Apple and Google report even greater gaps between average and high performers."

When high performers smash expectations, break production records, and develop award winning innovations that drive up company bottom line, how does this affect other employees? Could they become intimidated by the success and talent of the high performer? In the same article, Willyerd notes:

"This hypothesis might sound far-fetched, but it's actually common for peers to punish top performers. For instance, there is a long history of factory workers punishing peers for working "too fast." Peers tend not to like colleagues who are "rate-busters" because it may increase management's expectations of how much can be accomplished within a certain time, or for a certain pay."

Intimidation can also lead the low performer to avoid the high performer in multiple ways: in interaction, socialization, and collaboration to name a few. The low performer may be afraid that his or her work and/or talent may become marginalized or even ridiculed when compared to that of the high performer.

However, in such cases, the low performer may be a great candidate for a mentor-mentee relationship with the high performer. By helping the low performer see the high performer as a person who wants to help him or her improve, the uneasy feeling of intimidation may cease as they work together and get to know each other.

- High Performers can Burn Out Faster than Others

Do you remember the old commercials featuring the Energizer Bunny? The ads implied that, due to the powerful batteries, the toy bunny could just keep going and going forever. High performers are similar. Their energy and drive can seem unending as they consistently deliver day in day out.

Former CMO @Googleplay and Startup Founder Coach Patrick Mork, writes in a November 2017 article for Medium entitled, *How to Manage High Performers:*

"These people are like high performance sports cars. They'll drive at 12,000 RPM as long as possible until they're out of gas. The problem is that some of them will often blow the engine as a result (and burnout)."

Intense focus is a trademark of high performers and one of the reasons why they tend to accomplish higher productivity. When intense focus is mixed with elevated passion and stirred with exceptional drive to succeed, it can often lead to long weeks without enough rest and recuperation. While the

Energizer Bunny commercial may be cute, humans don't run off batteries. They cannot keep going and going without proper rest, relaxation, and nutrition.

The Rallyware blog has a July 2018 article entitled High-performers in the Workplace: How to Identify and Develop Your A-team that states this concerning high performers:

"If they're engulfed by the task they do, they won't notice how quickly time goes by. They will do late night calls concerning job-related issues and will be the first to come to the office. Such behavior is not episodic: it's their routine."

As the manager or leader of high performers, it's your job to help them avoid crashes. Depending upon them to recognize the need for physical, emotional, and mental rest may not be the wise thing to do. Often, they may be so focused and determined to complete a task or project that the warnings signs of a breakdown may escape their notice.

It would be appropriate for leaders to watch for warning signs of a pending crash such as out-of-character behavior (i.e., clashing with co-workers), reduction in performance without a good reason, or becoming irresponsible and uncaring about tasks and assignments.

To prevent burnout, leaders would be wise to *strongly* suggest that high performers who meet these criteria take time off. They may object because of their exceptional commitment. However, leaders should sternly remind them why the time is needed and the benefits of approaching tasks and projects from a refreshed state.

- High Performers can be More Susceptible to Arrogance

Author Manami Das of Christ University, Bangalore, is the author of an article for *ResearchGate* written in December 2015 entitled *Impact of Perceived Workplace Arrogance on Stress levels on employees.* It states:

"... Workplace Arrogance is a demeaning behavior which an individual exhibits in order to establish or demonstrate their superiority over others. This behavior affects the interpersonal relationships, causes increased stress in the employees, in addition to general occupational stress"

High performers' outstanding achievements are certainly worthy of the awards, recognition, and accolades they tend to receive. Their accomplishments are hard fought and any celebrations resulting from their dedication are well deserved and, hopefully, are received with humility by the high performer. But there may be times when high achievers develop a hint of arrogance and pride because of the superstar attention.

They know they are talented. They hear the compliments from leaders and managers. They see the results of their innovative ideas and how the company benefits from their hard work and contributions. The question becomes, *Will they take it all in with a humble attitude, or will they become arrogant and overestimate their value to the team and company?*

According to a February 2012 article written for Personnel Psychology entitled *The Best and the Rest: Revisiting the Norm of Normality of Individual Performance,* authors Ernest O'Boyle Jr. and Herman Aguinis notes 10% of productivity comes from the top 1% of employees and 26% of output is a product of the top 5%.

The best know they are the best. Being in the top

1% or the top 5% means being a part of an exclusive club with few members and this fact alone could foster arrogance. Humility and arrogance can underlie an employee's character and thinking and might be surface in their attitude toward others. There is no professional training course on how to be humble or how to avoid pride and arrogance. These are issues of the human heart and leaders should address them as such.

Therefore, leaders should be watchful for the signs of arrogance among high performers such as constantly demeaning other employees, asking for special favors or benefits that other employees do not have, and bragging or boasting about their accomplishments without acknowledging the contributions of other team members.

If any of these signs occur, managers should take the high performer aside and carefully speak to the heart of the person. Help him or her see the importance of others, the value of teamwork, and the fact that more talent does not equate to more employee value. In a nutshell, help him or her to understand and embrace the phrase;

"You may have more talent than others, but never more value as an employee."

* * *

Solutions for High Performer Unique Challenges

- Create a Rewards/Recognition System with Shared Resources

Some research shows that when other employees share in the rewards of high performers, peers feel less threatened. That is according to a controlled experiment on 284 U.S. business majors on how group members react to top performance. The article that sites this information was written in July 2015 by Francesca Gino for Scientific American and is entitled, The Problem with Being a top Performer. Part of it states:

"The results showed that star performers triggered different reactions from their peers depending on the resources available to the team. If resources were limited, peers felt threatened by and competitive toward high

performers and thus undermined them. If resources were shared, peers benefitted from working with a star and thus socially supported the high performer."

Leaders can rightfully conclude that selfishness can sabotage the work of high performers. It's the age-old question at work: *What do I get out of it?* If the high performer's hard work and achievements bring benefits to the group or team, then others will likely support him or her. If not, they will likely, at the least, withdraw any support, and at the most, sabotage the high performer's work.

This should not be surprising. It speaks to the real nature of human beings and is further verified by these words in the same article:

"We've seen that when we compare ourselves to others and fall short, envy can lead us to undermine them. But Campbell and colleagues' study suggests something even more sinister: peers resent and lash out against star achievers strategically—that is, only when it is not in their best interest to support them."

What's in it for me is, unfortunately, a driving force of

many employees. There are times when leaders should speak to the human nature of employees regarding certain characteristics (i.e. arrogance). But there are also times when it may be best to know what that nature is and use techniques that will guide that nature toward the benefit of the company. That is why leaders should implement a rewards and recognition system that brings benefits to all group and team members — not just to high performers.

- Convince co-workers to focus on cooperation rather than competition

The message and mentality of cooperation can be emphasized in multiple ways. Leaders can communicate the message by explicitly sharing the fact that every contribution, whether big or small, counts toward the end goal of a stronger team and increased company bottom line. Managers can also help employees recognize the benefits of collaborating with high performers: increased knowledge, exposure to high performer experiences, and the discovering of secrets to increased output.

By complimenting high performers instead of

competing against them, the benefits can outweigh the threats and managers can assure their star performers are embraced rather than sabotaged.

- Hold high performers accountable at the same level as others

High achievement should not be an excuse or cover for egregious behavior. All companies should have baselines of organizational values and high performers should not be allowed to operate outside of those baselines. Leaders should hold them accountable for straying from acceptable social interactions with their coworkers and management.

They should not be allowed to shrug off team norms, operate in a bubble, or behave counter to basic human values toward others which include decency and respect for all.

It can be tempting for leaders to turn a blind eye to high performer misbehavior because of their superior output performance. But managers and leaders can avoid this tendency by redefining the definition of high performer to include their treatment of others. This can be emphasized with the statement:

"A high performer can't just do better than others, they must also bring out the best in others."

By adding human interaction with talent and ability, leaders can send a strong message that everyone, high performer or otherwise, will be defined by how well they strengthen the team culture. This should help all employees see themselves in a well-rounded way.

As a leader, you may be familiar with these proposed solutions and have other methods you utilize in your workplace. By doing so, you acknowledge the need to keep your high performers on track and in alignment with the operations of the rest of the team. Only by doing so can you ensure continued increases in production and consistent team chemistry.

Self-Reflection
Understanding of My Unique Challenges

I understand the unique challenges of my high performers and have addressed/are addressing them.

[ ] Yes   [ ] No   [ ] Maybe

I am confident my lower level leaders understand the unique challenges of their high performers and have addressed them.

[ ] Yes   [ ] No   [ ] Maybe

I hold my leaders and high performers accountable for their social and professional behavior.
[ ] Yes   [ ] No   [ ] Maybe

Notes/Thoughts:

To-Dos:

7

Understanding of My Unique Personality

he Performance Development Group LLC. has an 2004 article entitled, *The Psychology of Top Performers.* The authors, Richard W. Molden and Steven M. Swavely, share insights of a study:

"The psychological factors and behavioral characteristics that make up top performers and which leads them towards their goals and on to success are all learnable. In this article, we've summarized the most critical

psychological and behavioral traits top performers possess..."

High performers are known to possess some unique personality traits. Some of those traits are discussed in the article and shared in the following chapter sections. When observing these traits, some leaders may mistakenly misinterpret high performer actions as being selfish or disingenuous. Also, given the shifting demographic composition of the workplace, managers can develop preconceived notions regarding different age groups such as baby boomers, millennials, and generation X.

Because we are all human, stereotypes and certain prejudices may exist regarding some personnel resulting in misunderstandings. These often lead to inaccurate conclusions that eventually hamper effective communication between leaders and employees.

Although most diversity training courses tend to cover at least a portion of human socialization, it is important that leaders of high performers become familiar with each employee's unique individual personality. This would help avoid misconceptions and misunderstandings in the workplace.

The remainder of this chapter is dedicated to identifying various personality traits that most high performers tend to exhibit. As you read, can you identify some of these traits in your existing high performers?

***

High Performer Personality Traits

- High Confidence

High confidence tends to manifest itself in stressful situations. High performers often possess the ability to calmly and rationally analyze and resolve problems without going into panic mode. This should be a valued trait to most managers but unfortunately some leaders tend to misinterpret the calm demeanor associated with high confidence as a lack of concern. They may think the high performer doesn't take the problem seriously.

For example, years ago I worked for a large organization whose IT department was in its infant stage of growth. As technology expanded so did the huge response-time requirements of applications. Whenever an unexpected network outage occurred, the CIO, known for his extreme reactions to unforeseen problems, came over to the cubicle of the network admin, hovered over him, and badgered him with questions and concerns as the admin worked to identify the issue. At one point, as the admin calmly looked through the error logs, the CIO suggested,

"Maybe you need to speed it up and act like you care..."

I'll never forget the admin's facial expression—one that suggested, "You may be in panic mode, but I'm not."

High performers exhibit confidence in the face of downed systems, slow performance, low sales, and other challenges. Yet, there is a difference between confidence and cockiness—the latter being a reckless and selfish attitude that eventually leads to disaster.

High performers know when to compromise on what they believe and when to stand firm on their convictions. They take risks and are brave when it comes to the area of the unknown. But these risks are carefully measured, not thoughtless and dangerous.

They tend to exude passion and positivity through a can-do attitude which is rooted in confidence. That, in turn, can motivate and bolster the morale and even the productivity of their co-workers—all without intentionally trying to do so.

One can say confidence is the X-factor of high performers and leaders should not mistake it for arrogance or egotism. Rather, confidence is a key ingredient for their success and the foundation for their innovative brainstorms.

- Quality over Quantity

Most high performers consider quality a higher priority than simply getting the task done. They tend to pay more attention to the details of the project—taking more time to make sure the I's are dotted and the T's are crossed. After all, their reputations are at stake and their work is on full display.

At times, leaders can mistakenly mistake their tedious processing for confusion or laziness when in fact they tend to be extremely focused and detailed. They also tend to live by the motto:

Do it right the first time, and you won't have to do it again.

Years ago, two of my co-workers who were programmers had a tense exchange about writing application programs. The high performer was complaining to a non-high performer about writing sloppy code—thereby creating a need to re-write the program. The non-high performer suggested there are many ways to code, and one could take the liberty to do it whatever way desired. The high performer spoke in a stern voice:

"What do you mean many ways? There's only one way, and that's the right way!"

This unwavering commitment to quality does have its disadvantages. Non-high performers tend to take exception to this character trait. Some of the names I've heard used during my career to describe high performers are *picky, selective,* and *anal.*

I worked as a quality control technician during an early occupation. My job was to inspect, then reject or pass newly built mainframe computers. It was a lonely job because most of my co-workers highly disliked QA (quality assurance) folks--as they called us. When I inspected and rejected someone's hard work, there was always a sentiment of:

Are you kidding me? You could have overlooked that!

There appears to be something inherently combative about ensuring quality among non-high performers. It could be the resistance of taking the extra time needed to verify correctness or the nonchalant attitude of just getting something done and off the table. However, high performers don't suffer with those shortcomings. They make sure their work is not only completed but done in the best way possible because their names are on the line.

- *Fearless Decision-Making*

Fearless does not mean high performers have no fear. Rather, they are not hindered by the fear of making mistakes. They will act despite fear. They tend to step up and make decisions when it's necessary— especially when there is a problem that should be resolved. They will make extraordinary efforts to create innovative solutions (assuming leaders have established this freedom as part of their company culture). They will live with the consequences and operate with the realization that the benefits far outweigh the risks.

Also, fearless does not mean reckless—having no back-up or back-out plan or making important high-risk decisions in a vacuum, on a whim, and without proper notification of necessary personnel. These actions represent immaturity and selfishness and are not beneficial to anyone in the company.

But when high performers take control when needed and make high-risk decisions in a responsible manner, they should be commended for assuming the leadership role, no matter the outcome, rather than condemned and accused of trying to usurp authority. Often, they take charge and delegate as needed because they see an opportunity to get something done or to resolve a problem.

- Self-Direction

Leaders do not have to push high performers to excel or to do the things necessary for professional growth.

High achievers are more likely to perform their own research, do their own testing, and reach their own conclusions through vigorous trial and error.

They tend to spend more time on projects than non-high performers and are self-motivated when it comes to new assignments and challenges. They also tend to seek out those in the organization who have the influence and knowledge needed to help them succeed.

As a caution, even self-direction can be abused if high performers are spending huge amounts of time on tasks or projects unrelated to their current assignments. Being self-directed is good only if it leads the employee to gain knowledge and experience that will enhance their area of expertise or improve their capacity to solve problems and create solutions in the workplace.

High performers will search out the latest courses and enroll in applicable training and certification programs because they desire to learn and grow. They have goals, plans, and a sense of a path to take on the road to fulfilling their desires for professional enhancement.

But their self-directed character can be seen by

managers as annoying—especially when it comes to company finances. It's usually high performers who request money for new material or training courses—setting off the ire of cash-strapped leaders with tiny department budgets. Though the reality of low funding is real for many managers, they should seek ways to satisfy the learning desires of high performers—knowing their professional improvement could translate into a bottom-line increase or more effective support for company and application issues.

A couple of those alternative education methods could be sending one employee to training and tasking him or her to teach other employees. Also, bringing vendors and teachers onsite to teach a group of employees is a great lower cost solution for education.

- Desire for Autonomy

Most high performers are curious and open-minded. These are character traits that can lead them to out-of-the-box solutions. As a result, they crave a responsible level of autonomy—the freedom to operate outside of the box, and at times, to rip the traditional box apart and completely redesign the damn thing!

Through their vast array of talent and creativity, they can develop savvy but unconventional solutions that, frankly, can strike fear in some leaders. Most managers made it to their positions not because they took high risks but because they followed company rules and expectations. Therefore, one can understand why non-traditional solutions tend to spook some managers.

But most high performers acknowledge the status quo and authority figures yet are unafraid to respectfully challenge traditional boundaries and beliefs of how things are done in the company. If leaders embrace the granting of autonomy, this can lead to solving age-old problems as well as discovering new innovative solutions.

Book Summary

Now that you have read, processed, and ingested this information, it's up to you to port it into your world and into the worlds of those working for you. There is a popular saying: *Knowledge is Power.* But I say,

"Power is only effective if it leads to change."

Will this book change the way you think, plan, and practice your leadership? Will it lead you to re-evaluate not only your practices but the mentalities of those working for you? Most of all, will it lead to positive changes for your high performers and other employees?

My desire for you is to be successful in all you do — in business and in life. May you excel in all your hands find to do.

Self-Reflection

Understanding of My Unique Personality

I can identify some of these character traits in my high performers.

[ ] Yes   [ ] No   [ ] Maybe

I am confident that all levels of management below me can identify some of these character traits in their high performers.

[ ] Yes   [ ] No   [ ] Maybe

I have granted my leaders and my high performers a certain level of autonomy and I trust them to handle it in a responsible manner.

[ ] Yes   [ ] No   [ ] Maybe

Notes/Thoughts:

To-Dos:

Author Biography

Charles Lee Holley (C.L. Holley) is an Inspirational Speaker, Author, and Business professional with the unique background of Technology, Business, and Counseling. Born the youngest of seventeen in north Alabama during the civil rights movement, and as a

child of severe poverty, he suffered from a speech impediment called stuttering and was terrified to speak in public. But through faith and determination to overcome, he became the first in his family to graduate from college—earning a B.S. in Business Administration and a Master of Biblical Counseling as well as numerous technology certifications. After marrying his college sweetheart, tragedy struck with the sudden death of his teenage son. Drowning in depression, he penned his first book about the death of his son entitled When Flowers Fade. To date, he has written numerous books and is a dynamic Toastmasters International Speaker who shares inspiration and information on a variety of topics.

Business Services Offered

- **Leaders-Sharpening-Leaders** Power Luncheon
- Employee Engagement Improvement (Consulting)
- Keynote Speaker
- Conference Speaker
- Workshop Speaker
- Special Events Speaker
- Business, Education, and Faith Based Organizations

For more information, cost, and discounts, please visit SpeakerHolley.com **or send email with requests to** SpeakerHolley@gmail.com.

Follow the author on social media (SpeakerHolley) and register on the website for notification of new books, services, and events.

Thanks for reading! **Please add a short review** on Amazon and let the author know if this book added value to your leadership skill set!

Review: https://www.amazon.com/dp/B082VLFKJH

Link: https://www.amazon.com/dp/B07NKRF97H

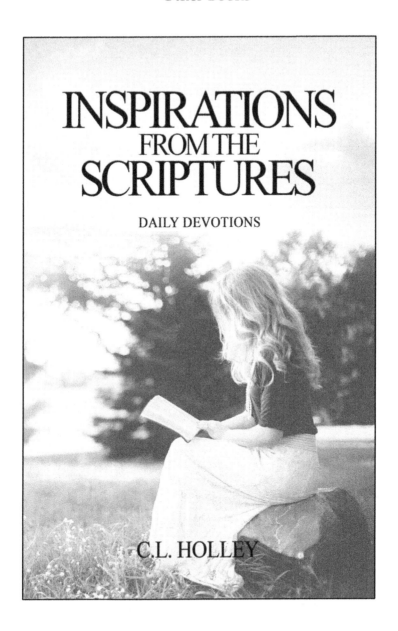

Link: https://www.amazon.com/dp/B07NK8HH4G

Link: https://www.amazon.com/dp/1798490706

Online Links for Referenced Resources

Introduction

https://www.forbes.com/sites/johnhall/2019/02/24/how-you-can-keep-high-performers-loyal-to-your-company/#752f50aa7aa7

Chapter One

https://hbr.org/2007/05/why-employees-are-afraid-to-speak

Chapter Two

https://www.strategy-business.com/article/re00160?gko=09516
https://hbr.org/2019/04/research-why-managers-ignore-employees-ideas

Chapter Three

https://www.shrm.org/hr-today/trends-and-forecasting/research-and-surveys/Documents/2016-Employee-Job-Satisfaction-and-Engagement-Report.pdf

https://www.shrm.org/hr-today/trends-and-forecasting/research-and-surveys/pages/job-satisfaction-and-engagement-report-revitalizing-changing-workforce.aspx

https://www.inc.com/michael-schneider/8-years-of-neuro-research-shows-you-how-to-increase-employee-productivity-by-50-percent-with-1-initiative.html

https://www.govexec.com/management/2018/01/almost-70-us-managers-are-scared-talk-their-employees/144986/

https://www.milkbusiness.com/article/giving-employees-more-responsibility-has-both-benefits-and-drawbacks

https://www.shrm.org/resourcesandtools/hr-topics/organizational-and-employee-development/pages/delegateeffectively.aspx

Chapter Four

https://www.forbes.com/sites/johnhall/2019/02/24/how-you-can-keep-high-performers-loyal-to-your-company/#752f50aa7aa7

http://www.incentivemag.com/Resources/Research/Co-Workers-Are-Most-Important-Factor-for-Workplace-Happiness/

Chapter Five

https://www.broadcenter.org/blog/high-performers/

https://www.hrdive.com/news/why-are-your-top-performers-leaving/546023/

https://www.rallyware.com/blog/high_performers_in_the_workplace_how_to_identify_and_develop_your_a_team

Chapter Six

https://www.rallyware.com/blog/high_performers_in_the_workplace_how_to_identify_and_develop_your_a_team

https://onlinelibrary.wiley.com/doi/full/10.1111/j.1744-6570.2011.01239.x

https://www.aib.edu.au/blog/leadership/challenges-high-performing-employees/

https://www.scientificamerican.com/article/the-problem-with-being-a-top-performer/

https://hbr.org/2014/11/what-high-performers-want-at-work

https://medium.com/swlh/how-to-manage-high-performers-c51dbfca3e31

https://www.researchgate.net/publication/298951345_Impact_of_Perceived_Workplace_Arrogance_on_Stress_levels_on_empl
oyees

https://www.forbes.com/sites/markmurphy/2018/07/01/3-reasons-why-high-performers-are-often-miserable/#3ae5cbaa45fc

Chapter Seven

http://competitive-streak.com/pdf/WP%20Psychology%20of%20Top%20Performers%20.pdf

https://www.thehartford.com/business-insurance/strategy/employee-performance/traits-top-employees

Made in the USA
Monee, IL
11 February 2020

21625177R00069